G000097793

Hello there!

Hello there!

The life and times of
ANTHONY BEARD
'The Wag from Widecombe'

WENDY BEARD
with Sue Viccars

Foreword by Rob Steemson

BLACKINGSTONE
PUBLISHING

DEDICATION

To Sidney and Florence Beard, Anthony's father and mother,
for producing such a lovely son

First published 2019
Published by Blackingstone Publishing
2 Steward Cottages Moretonhampstead Devon TQ13 8SD

© Wendy Beard 2019

The right of Wendy Beard to be identified as Author of this work has been
asserted in accordance with the Copyrights, Designs and Patents Act 1988.

Photographs courtesy of the Beard family unless otherwise acknowledged. Every
effort has been made to trace the copyright holders of photographs, but in some
cases this has proved impossible. The authors and publisher apologise for any
inconsistencies in this respect. Note that some material in this book has previously
been published in *Dartmoor Magazine*.

Edited by Sue Viccars, Blackingstone Publishing
Designed by Emily Kingston

All rights reserved. No part of this book may be reprinted or reproduced or utilised
in any form or by any electronic, mechanical or other means, now known or
hereafter invented, including photocopying and recording, or in any information
storage or retrieval system, without the permission in writing from the Publishers.

British Library Cataloguing in Publication Data
A catalogue record for this book is available from the British Library.

ISBN 978-0-9954986-2-4

Typesetting and origination by Blackingstone Publishing
Printed in Great Britain by Short Run Press, Exeter, Devon

Front cover At Chagford Show PHOTOGRAPH ALAN QUICK
Back cover At a Totnes Young Farmers' dinner and dance
PHOTOGRAPH REGINALD A. BAKER PRESS AND COMMERCIAL
PHOTOGRAPHY, EXETER

CONTENTS

Anthony commentating at Widecombe Fair in 2009

FOREWORD

It was a fantastic surprise but also a great honour to be asked by Anthony Beard's family to provide the Foreword to Wendy's book. I would therefore like to take this opportunity to share with you some personal memories about this very knowledgeable, positive, inspirational, trusting and passionate gentleman, a 'gentle man' that I had the privilege of knowing all my life.

The saying goes 'Behind every successful man there is a good woman', and that person is most definitely Wendy. She was Anthony's granite rock, and with their two sons Stephen and Trevor they had a very happy family life together. Wendy also had her own job as the Secretary at Widecombe-in-the-Moor Primary School. It is with gritty determination and real focus that she has been able to write this fantastic insight into Anthony's early years, and their fifty-six years of marriage and family life.

I remember the phone call from friend Lloyd Mortimore informing me about Anthony's passing. I was birdwatching with my family at Berry Head. It seemed fitting that from where I stood near the cliff edge I could look up towards the overcast moor. It was a very sad moment, and one I recall every time I return to this part of the coast.

Anthony was well known across Devon and beyond as 'The Wag from Widecombe'. He was born and bred in the parish of Widecombe-in-the-Moor, and was known locally as the 'Widecombe Wag'. He had a very deep love of and pride in Devon, Dartmoor and particularly Widecombe, and a very strong commitment to community involvement. He had a fantastically captivating demeanour and could always be relied upon to help out if he could.

My mother and Anthony went to Widecombe Primary School together and had a close friendship throughout their respective lives and careers in the local community. He was a dairy farmer and local milkman, who delivered 400 pints over a sixteen-mile daily trip. My mother, after a few years of teaching, came home to run the village shop in Poundsgate. Apart from running a farm Anthony had already become an accomplished entertainer who just loved to make people laugh. When he got to the shop, about halfway on his round – and quite often over a coffee – he would test out some new jokes, making locals and visitors alike roar with laughter.

The unpasteurised milk was delivered in robust see-through plastic bags which always took some explaining to visitors. I can recall one visitor asking Anthony, 'Is this milk fresh?' His quick retort was, 'Of course tiz missus, this yer milk was grass only a couple of hours ago!'

Anthony's life in the entertainment world started at Widecombe in 1965, when he (and a couple of other local people) set up an amateur dramatic society called the Moorland Merrymakers, which is still going today. Soon after, he was invited to 'speak for his supper' at the annual Dartmoor Whiteface Sheep Breeders' dinner in Ashburton, and a whole new career snowballed. His sharp humour and wit, and the ability to make people laugh, are also well documented through his work at BBC Radio Devon, particularly the Sunday request show and *Dartmoor Diary*. I recall vividly my first live radio broadcast was on the *Dartmoor Diary* programme and he put me at ease by saying, 'Just tell us as it is on the ground, boy!'

From the Dartmoor National Park Authority's perspective, Anthony helped us on many community-based occasions, particularly those involving nature and archaeology, and was an extremely entertaining after-dinner speaker at conferences. He was closely involved with our fiftieth anniversary celebrations in 2001, and at our sixtieth he kindly offered to oversee a Dartmoor quiz which we hosted with Parish Council members from all over the moor. He was also a staunch supporter of the DNPA Local History Day – chairing the annual meeting of all the local community history groups.

In Widecombe, Anthony had been a Parish Councillor and was a long-standing member of the Widecombe Fair Committee. He was instrumental in starting the Widecombe History Group in 1997 and was an excellent Secretary. He thoroughly enjoyed receiving interesting letters and emails and requests for information from across the world. He was also very proud of, and shared with others, his large collection of artefacts – medieval pottery, prehistoric arrowheads and flints – found on the farm over many years.

To me, he was a fantastic mentor and showed the importance of being actively involved in a community. He was the voice of common sense on all countryside and rural matters. Great examples of this appeared on the final page of many issues of the *Dartmoor Magazine*.

With greatest respect I would like to use one of Anthony's jokes, which to me really sums up his general attitude to life. When a visitor to Widecombe asked him, 'Have you lived here all your life?', his response came razor-sharp: 'No not yet!'

Widecombe, Dartmoor and Devon have lost a great ambassador and friend who enriched the lives of so many people. I am aware of how much I still miss Anthony's presence and can now record my thanks for those memories and laughter. Thank you, Wendy, for undertaking this project which will bring back so many happy memories for so many people: a fantastic accomplishment and a great tribute to everything Anthony achieved throughout his very rewarding life.

ROB STEEMSON

Community & Landscape Management Ranger

Dartmoor National Park

At Rob and Kathryn's wedding at the Two Bridges Hotel, 10 June 2006

INTRODUCTION

On a crisp, bright and sunny Saturday in late January 2017 more than a thousand people gathered at the Cathedral Church of St Peter in Exeter for a very special occasion: to celebrate the life of (and I quote from the cover of the service sheet) 'Tony Beard – The Wag from Widecombe'.

I came into the story quite late on, first meeting Anthony (or Tony, as I knew him from his public persona) in the spring of 2005 when I became, for a year or two, editor of 'another' Dartmoor magazine (long since gone). For that magazine 'Tony' Beard was writing the 'Tailpiece', which appeared on the final page. So when I was lucky enough to become editor of *Dartmoor Magazine* in the autumn of 2008 one of the first things I wanted to do was get Tony back on board – and so from then until winter 2015 he once again had the 'Last Word' in every issue, regaling readers with a series of entertaining stories and memories, everything from rabbiting and mole-catching and rural public transport (or, rather, the lack of it) to local characters and the need for common sense and the tedium of 'health and safety'. While working on this book I've gone back through my records and have re-read many, many of Tony's 'Last Words' (extracts from some appear on these pages). They reveal so much: his love for and deep understanding of rural life, of Devon, of Dartmoor, and of Widecombe in particular; his knowledge of everybody and everything in the local area; his ability to recall the past without falling into the 'rose-coloured spectacles' trap.

Wendy first sent me her manuscript a year or so ago, and I was immediately struck by the personal story she had to tell of her life with Anthony. I went to see her at Bittleford Parks, and as we chatted and looked through the family photograph albums I realised that there was a lot more to say. That's the joy of oral history: what starts out as a relaxed chat over a cup of coffee, pouring over some old pictures, can lead to pure gold. I have enjoyed every minute of working on this book with Wendy – it has been a real privilege.

And so to the title: Tony, or Anthony? On talking to Wendy it was obvious ('I don't know what his mother would have thought – he was *always* Anthony!'). And so it was at home, and in the family, and to his friends… the wider world may have known him as 'Tony', but this is, essentially, a book about family, and friends, and life in Widecombe.

So let's celebrate the life and times of Anthony Beard – a very special man.

SUE VICCARS

Editor *Dartmoor Magazine*

Moretonhampstead, July 2019

View over Widecombe-in-the-Moor from the Hameldown ridge

LIFE AND TIMES

Early Years

My dear mother said of Anthony when she first met him, 'He has been given a great gift.' I have never forgotten that statement, and when I look back on his life, I can understand what she was saying.

here have been Beards in Widecombe parish for generations – at least as far back as the early eighteenth century. I have a copy of the family tree – written on an old roll of wallpaper! – showing that Mark Beard, born in 1730, married Elizabeth Leyman in 1755. The earliest family marriage certificate we have dates from 1853, when Anthony's great-grandfather, William Beard, shoemaker of Ponsworthy, married Elizabeth Hamlyn White, of Sherwill. Anthony too was born in the parish, in the house where we lived together and where I still live.

Widecombe-in-the-Moor is a large parish on Dartmoor, the village nestling beneath the Hameldown ridge. The northern end is marked by a small hamlet, Natsworthy, about three miles from the village centre, up a very narrow and winding lane. The boundary on the west follows the Wallabrook, the East Dart and then the 'Double Dart'; on the east it crosses Bonehill Down. From Widecombe village the centre of Ponsworthy is roughly two miles away and Poundsgate about another two miles further on, from where the road drops downhill to Newbridge spanning the River Dart, a very popular beauty spot. Widecombe was made famous by the traditional folksong

ABOVE Anthony's mother's parents: Granny and Granfer John Knight Grills
ABOVE RIGHT Anthony's grandmother Annie (née Palmer), was born in 1887 and married Ernest Beard in 1903. This photograph shows Annie's mother wearing the family locket, 1890s

Anthony's grandfather, Ernest, around 1900

TOP Sidney and Florence courting on the moor in the early 1930s
ABOVE Anthony's father, Sidney (left, born 1911) with a friend, around 1920
ABOVE RIGHT Sidney and Florence's wedding in Torquay, 25 April 1935 (I think that the carpets over the wall behind them were put there to provide a more suitable backdrop!)

Anthony at two months old, in his christening robe, with his mother Florence (our sons Stephen and Trevor wore that robe when they were christened)

'Widecombe Fair', telling the story of Tom Pearce and his grey mare ('and Uncle Tom Cobley 'n all'), which was rediscovered by the Revd Sabine Baring-Gould in the late nineteenth century (the Wikepedia entry about 'Widecombe Fair', states 'Tony Beard, a member of the local history group that has researched the song, says "I'm convinced the characters were real people", concluding that they are likely to have been inhabitants of the Spreyton area [north of the moor] and that the song may commemorate an event that happened in 1802).

Anthony Ernest came into the world on 6 April 1936, born to Florence and Sidney Beard of Bittleford Parks Farm, Widecombe-in-the-Moor. His mother, born in 1905, came from Torquay and was a housemaid to Colonel and Mrs Hankey of Leusdon Lodge, Poundsgate. His father, Sidney, born in 1911, lived with his elder brother Wilfred, father Ernest and mother Annie at Ponsworthy village grocery shop. Ernest used to deliver groceries, including paraffin, to all the surrounding areas in his big van, as well as dealing in horses and running a carriage hire business. Ponsworthy was a self-sufficient village in those days, and only a few miles from Leusdon Lodge. Sidney and Florence were married in April 1935 and moved directly to Bittleford Parks to live in a newly built bungalow which served as the farmhouse (as it still does today).

TOP Florence feeding chickens on the farm, 1935
ABOVE Anthony at one month old. He was born twelve months after Florence and Sidney married

Anthony was an only child. Although most births took place at home at that time, he was born in Torbay Hospital due to complications. His parents

Anthony with his father at Bittleford Parks on his first birthday, 6 April 1937

had hoped for more children, but it was not possible; his mother was never in good health, so naturally he was very precious to them. Florence was a lovely lady and had a great influence on his early years: she only had to give him a 'look'! She never smacked him (and that said it all), but she was full of fun and she insisted he was called Anthony, *never* Tony. She taught him to read and write before going to school (and she had the same influence over our two sons, Stephen and Trevor, many years later).

Anthony's father worked hard on the farm and was dogged with bad luck as Florence had to have a big operation soon after they were married. Anthony also fell very ill when he was five years old and a Dr Williams was sent for from London, who diagnosed glandular fever. He prescribed medicine, and Anthony recovered. To settle these big bills Sidney had to sell some cattle (he had to pay his wife's bill within twenty-four hours of her operation), so life became very hard.

Just down the road from Bittleford Parks, in another bungalow ('Merrypark'), lived Anthony's Uncle Wilfred Beard and Aunty Gwendoline (*née* French), together with their son David (Anthony's cousin, younger

Wilfred Beard (Anthony's uncle, born 1905), Florence and Sidney outside Merrypark Garage in the early 1930s. You can see Sidney blowing his cheeks out – he was quite a comic!

The wedding of Wilfred Beard and Gwendoline French in 1932 (Sidney is on the right). Gwen came from Poundsgate, and the wedding took place at St John the Baptist Church, Leusdon

Uncle Wilfred with a car decked out for a wedding, 1930s

by fifteen months). As David (who died in 2017) said many years later, 'Anthony and I were brought up next door to one another, both only children and with no other playmates, so we were more like brothers than cousins in those early years. I too was actively involved in everything he got up to, from mole catching to entertaining… I was best man at his wedding and he was mine, too.' They remained very close throughout their lives.

Wilfred and Gwen ran a very successful garage business at Merrypark, selling petrol, running school buses and taxis, and a bus service from Widecombe to Ashburton and Newton Abbot via Ponsworthy and Poundsgate. At the same time the Potter family ran Tor Buses from Widecombe to Newton Abbot via Haytor, Liverton and Ilsington.

Ernest Beard, Anthony's grandfather, sometime in the 1940s. He was a fine old chap – over six feet tall – and kept his hair right up until he died!

A beautiful studio portrait of Anthony at four years old in 1940

There were lots of these rural bus services back then.

I remember the garage as a hub of activity, a centre for people to meet and collect their newspapers which the school bus driver brought back from Ashburton each day. Repairs were also carried out there. This wonderful service was sorely missed for many years after it closed.

Anthony had a normal rural village life until the age of eleven. He had a great playmate in David, and also in Frederick Trant, a farmer's son who lived on the next-door farm towards Ponsworthy. The head teacher at Widecombe-in-the-Moor Primary School was a Mrs Tucker (Anthony missed the first year because of his illness). He never got on with her particularly well. He told me how she shut him in the stationery cupboard at one time, and how he picked up a pile of those sticky coloured squares used in art class and tore them into strips. Miss Tweed taught the infant class. Mr Thorpe of Bonehill House ran the Boy Scouts group in the village, and through this Anthony learned all the usual important tasks that this organisation had to offer, and that boys his age needed to know.

'Health & Safety'. That will be our downfall before long, I can tell 'ee. 'You learn by your own mistakes' was a good old saying that has lasted for years.

We all climbed trees, sometimes we fell out of them. It didn't stop us; we held on tighter next time. We played conkers. Not now you don't, you may hit the other kid's thumb and that will never do!

We all had a 'pocket knife', with no thought of doing any harm with it. The only one that may get cut was yourself, and you soon learnt to respect the tool you were handling. What a world opened up, with a little bit of whittling on a piece of wood. Get a piece of sycamore about four inches long, cut a small ring out of the bark, remove the rest in one piece and then carve out a couple of notches, put back the bark and you had a whistle. No expense, and when it stopped working make another – great fun. I think 'twas called 'improvisation'!

No Boy Scout was properly dressed without a pocket or sheath knife. It was the country boy's tool, with so many uses: paunch a rabbit, skin a mole, cut up an apple or peel a carrot. I'm sure we all built up an immunity to lots of problems by not being too clean. A lovely old neighbour told me, 'You've got to eat a peck o' dirt during your life, but there's no need to eat the whole bl**** lot in one day!'

Was this the belief that immunisation was a gradual natural process? The cure for smallpox was found by noticing that dairy maids never caught the disease. The little blisters on cows' teats, now called cowpox, occasionally burst during the hand-milking process, and this gave those people, unknowingly, immunity by natural contact. I do wonder how many other cures are still to be discovered within the realms of nature that could help many modern complaints.

Folklore cures then come to mind – what a fascinating subject that is. When I was a little boy I had whooping cough. My father rounded up his flock of sheep and got them 'all steamed up and panting' and made me stand in the middle, inhaling their hot steamy breath. Did it do me any good? Well I'm still here today so it didn't do me any harm! 'Health & Safety' would go bananas just at the thought of it.

'Last Word' *Dartmoor Magazine* winter 2009

At eleven years old all children took the 11-plus exam. From Widecombe children went either to Ashburton Secondary School, as it was then, or King Edward VI Grammar School in Totnes, or Totnes High School for Girls. Devon County Council at that time awarded scholarships for public school places each year to the top three pupils sitting the 11-plus in Devon. Anthony, having been one of the three highest passes, was offered a place at Plymouth College: but as a boarder, because of the distance involved in getting there each day. He had only been to Plymouth once before, on his uncle's bus at Christmastime to see the pantomime, so knew nothing of the college or its whereabouts.

So at eleven years old he became a pupil there and boarded in a large house at Ford Park with about twenty other boys. It must have been a very traumatic time for him, being left at the college by his father and told he would be there for eight weeks before coming home, but I know that he came to like being there. It was a rugby, hockey and cricket college – football matches were taboo! – and I often heard him talk about the time he absconded one Saturday to watch Plymouth Argyle play. A roll call was made at lunchtime, and of course he was missing: 'Where were you, Beard, at lunchtime?' I know that he owned up and was duly given 'four of the best', bent over one of those old-fashioned radiators! He only did that once!

Music was also part of the curriculum: he learnt to play the cello and was in the school orchestra, as well as acting in Shakespeare plays. All the boarders were taken on long walks over Dartmoor at the weekend, including visits to Burrator Reservoir, Yelverton, Meavy and so on, covering many miles. I know he enjoyed his time at Plymouth and made several friends, and I'm sure the experience helped build him into the character he became.

Anthony (right) during his Plymouth College days, 1949

At sixteen he took his School Certificate and after doing well in the science subjects was offered a good career with Imperial Chemical Industries, but he decided to come home and help his parents to build up the farm. It was a big crossroads in his life, but he often told me he never regretted his decision. Anthony had realised the many sacrifices his parents had made for him, so he wanted to try and repay them

Plymouth College's Christmas play – Shakespeare's *Macbeth* – in 1951 (Anthony is second from right)

for all their love and attention – and of course, I would never have met him had he chosen the other road offered to him.

During his childhood he also found a fascination for anything to do with nature and the countryside, and it stayed with him all his life.

As a country boy I never had any weekly 'pocket money'; if you wanted something you had to earn it. Helping on the farm didn't count, that was part of being a farmer's son. So to earn a few pennies I caught rabbits and moles. I kept a couple of ferrets and about thirty handmade rabbit nets and weekends would set off with a sandwich or two in me pocket, rabbiting! Mother and Father wouldn't worry as long as I was back in time to feed the calves and help with the milking, Often I'd put the ferret into the hole one too many times. The poor old thing was tired and he would 'lie up' – go to sleep – and the problems would begin. There was only one thing for it, leave the ferret box and a little bread and milk near the hole and hope. Go back late evening and with luck he would be curled up sound asleep in the box and all was well.

A man, I think it was Mr Hill, came around twice a week and bought the rabbits. He sent them off from Moretonhampstead railway station to towns and cities all over the country for housewives to supplement their meagre meat ration. If a housewife had half a crown [12.5p] or three shillings [15p] she could buy a rabbit without using her meat ration coupons. Just think what she could do with that, a stew, a pie, a roast dinner, she was so resourceful.

'Last Word' *Dartmoor Magazine* spring 2014

Talking of rabbits – we would often find a rabbit's nest hole out in the middle of the field. No deeper than an arm's length. Lined with grass and fur from the female's breast and hidden away from the predators that generally followed the hedges in their pursuit of a meal. I can remember that if we found one with young in it we would send a message to Great Uncle John Hannaford at Headland, possibly one of the last of Dartmoor's warreners (rabbit farmers). He would arrive on his faithful Dartmoor pony with a large hessian sack over his shoulders and take the young rabbits back to his home and distribute them around his warren to introduce fresh bloodlines. A simple act which reduced the possibility of too much inbreeding and helped maintain a healthy breeding stock.

'Last Word' *Dartmoor Magazine* autumn 2015

Great Uncle John Hannaford (who lived at Headland Warren Farm) with Anthony in 1948. Anthony's grandmother Annie moved there from London as a child. Her mother had died, and her father's new wife didn't want her around, so she was sent to Headland Warren to be brought up by John and his wife

Anthony's collection of finds. In the small box in the centre (top) is a medieval lead 'Papal Bull', given to him by a fellow pupil at Plymouth College

Anthony was only six years old when, with his cousin David, checking the mole traps set the night before (he earned a bit of money by skinning the moles, drying and stretching the skins and posting them off to Horace Friend in Wisbech, Cambridgeshire for the fur trade) he noticed an object on top of a molehill. He realised that it looked different from other stones and asked his father what it might be. Sidney suggested a visit to a neighbouring farmer, Hermon French, who was very knowledgeable in geology, astronomy and prehistoric finds on Dartmoor. Hermon told him that what he was holding in his hand was at least three thousand years old.

I was thinking t'other day of the different people who influenced me when I was young. Hermon French was one. He was a farmer and, like me today, had a lot of outside interests. Geology, archaeology, astronomy, natural history and much more. His

enthusiasm rubbed off on me, and I'll tell 'ee how and why…

Once when I was about six years old my father had sown a field of oats, undersown it with grass seeds then rolled the field down – job done. When we woke next morning 'Mr and Mrs Mole' had had a wonderful time during the night and there were mole runs everywhere. I can remember Father now saying: 'Look what that naughty mole has done!' (English translation!).

I took my mole traps, knelt down beside one of the runs and beside my right knee was a beautiful flint arrowhead. I showed it to Hermon. He tried to explain to a six-year-old boy that the flint arrowhead was 3000 years old (made by hand a thousand years before the birth of Christ – phew!). This interested me so much that ever since I have been collecting prehistoric artefacts. The oldest I have dates from 8000BC. An interest in geology followed: granite and its associated quartz crystals, limestone with its fossils, stalagmites and stalactites. Natural history, mammals, mini beasts, flora and fauna, wonders all around to appreciate.

'Last Word' *Dartmoor Magazine* spring 2014

That find set Anthony on the road to a lifetime of interest in the history and archaeology of the area, particularly around Widecombe, resulting, as he said, in a wonderful collection of flint arrowheads, knives, scrapers, spindle whorls and so on: his 'treasures'. He always took great pleasure in sharing his 'finds' with other folk and used to take his collection with him when giving talks, letting people not only look at, but also touch and feel them. He also found discarded clay pipes – one particular favourite was in the shape of the devil's head, which his father ploughed up – and these formed part of his collection. He always seemed to have an 'eye' for finding objects when walking on the moors, and in December 1965 he had an article about his hobby published in *The Young Farmer* magazine.

LIFE AND TIMES

The Young Farmers' Club

When Anthony left school and came home to live and work on the farm at Bittleford Parks when he was sixteen, Peter Hicks, a neighbouring farmer, encouraged him to join the Newton Abbot Young Farmers' Club. He had never been a great mixer in his youth, particularly with girls; Plymouth College was a boys' only school and, never having a sister or close female cousin, he was very shy.

He soon became a firm member of the club and was encouraged to take part in public speaking, debating and drama competitions, as well as speaking at their annual dinner and dance evenings. It wasn't long before he became Secretary of the club.

He owes the YFC organisation so very much, as it brought him out of his shell. He got involved with stock-rearing classes, and then the National Proficiency Test Scheme tests came into being with various classes such as poultry killing, poultry trussing, shearing, hoeing and so on, with cooking, butter making, sewing, knitting and the like for the girls (I was a member of Totnes YFC). We had to pass an exam in each subject; more often than not a Miss Milner was the examiner, a lady not to be taken lightly. 'Tug' Wilson was the County Organiser, a man brilliant at motivating young people.

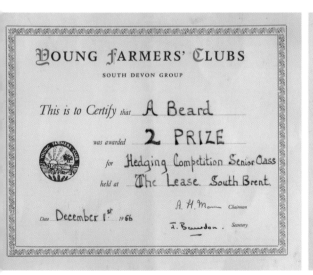
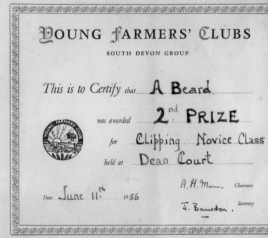

ABOVE Anthony entered lots of competitions. The certificates are signed by Jane Bawdon (now Dracup), who farms in Widecombe with her husband Peter – she belonged to Bovey Tracey Young Farmers; the chairman, Arthur Mann, was from Bovey Tracey
OPPOSITE TOP Anthony (left) as Learner Judge for fat sheep (reared for the butcher) at Newton Abbot Fat Stock Show, Christmas 1955
RIGHT At Ashburton Autumn Cattle Show in the mid-1950s: Anthony (second left) as Learner Judge for roots, with Messrs Marshall, Churchward (Judge), Marshall and Baskerville

ABOVE YFC Root Hoeing Proficiency Test at Bourton Farm (Totnes) in the mid-1950s: test passed! Anthony is in the back row, far left; Ruth is third from left, and I am standing to her left
LEFT Anthony being presented with a cup for the Essay Competition at Newton Abbot YFC Dinner and Dance by Maj. Gen. R.F. Cornwall (General Secretary BFYFC), about 1955. He was so thrilled – he was never that good at English!

When I was looking through our family photos I came across this lovely one of members of Totnes YFC having passed their root hoeing proficiency test – I'm in the front row, next to Ruth, my twin sister. Anthony's in the back row, on the far left. The funny thing was that he failed the test first time round, so had to come down to Totnes and re-take it with us! How anyone could fail a hoeing test beats me… it must have been quite a laugh at the time. I passed first time, even though I'd never done it before – my Dad didn't agree with girls being on the land.

Passes in these proficiency tests started with the award of a white bar, followed by various colours leading to silver and finally gold on reaching nine passes. I still have some of my bars, each one inscribed with 'WS' on the back. We both managed to achieve this and received our gold badges at the YFC Annual General Meeting

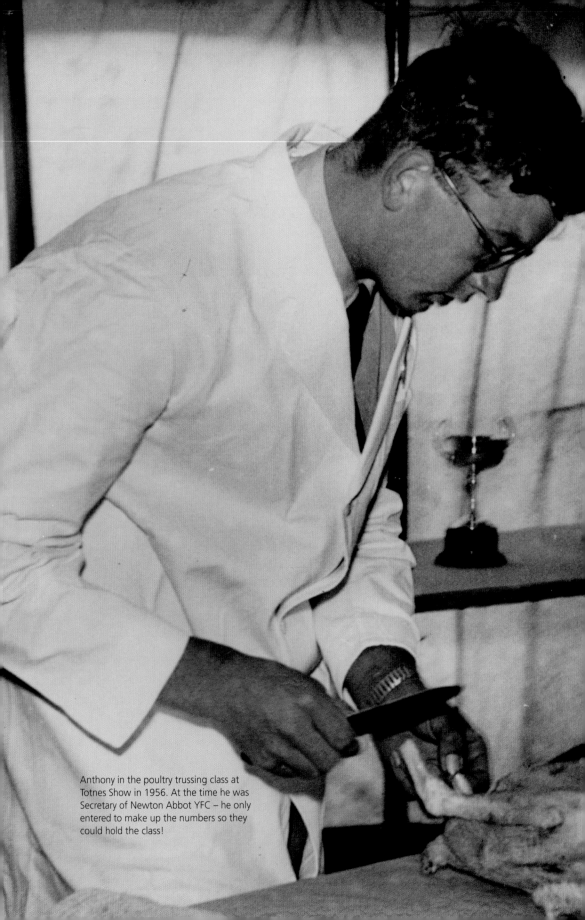

Anthony in the poultry trussing class at Totnes Show in 1956. At the time he was Secretary of Newton Abbot YFC – he only entered to make up the numbers so they could hold the class!

in London in 1958, a really great occasion. I remember we travelled up by train, and stayed in a hotel near Piccadilly Circus.

The YFC regional groups were made up of four or five different clubs. Newton Abbot belonged to the South Devon Group along with Totnes, South Brent, Bovey Tracey and Chagford. (It's interesting to remember that when reaching the age of twenty-five members were considered too old to be a 'young' farmer, and of course, most were married by then!) We all had our own dinners and dances and used to support each other's events.

I was brought up on a farm at Dartington with my parents Kenneth and Adeline – who both came from large farming families – my elder brother Kenneth George and my twin sister Ruth. Being a member of the Totnes YFC I was very involved with the events of the group. In 1956 Newton Abbot invited Totnes to their annual Christmas Party held at the Bradley Hotel in Newton Abbot, and that is where I first met Anthony. I can still see him now in a green tweed suit and trilby hat. The YFC was known to be something of a marriage bureau (as it is still today)!

On our trip to London in 1958 for the YFC awards

My gold YFC Craftsman badge

Adeline Horton (my mother, 1920s), was the second daughter in a farming family of five children

ABOVE Kenneth Selleck (my father, seen here in the 1920s) was the third son in a large farming family
ABOVE RIGHT Kenneth George (aged seven), my twin sister Ruth and me (aged two) in 1939

Anthony on his AGS motorbike at
Bittleford Parks in June 1956

We just seemed to 'click', and from then on we met each other at weekends and on Wednesdays when he came to Newton Abbot market with calves and pigs.

Anthony had an AGS motorbike at that time and could be heard roaring up through Dartington. He was very fond of this motorbike (Stephen tells me his Dad used to say that he could go up Widecombe Hill in third gear on that bike, but that it 'made a helluva racket'!). I'm not sure that my mother was too happy about me going on it (I didn't go on it that often), but she always loved it when he turned up; he was always full of fun and 'crams', and she enjoyed hearing all the news about Widecombe. Eventually he sold the bike and bought a blue A35 van, and later a new red Austin mini car.

I worked as Secretary to the Finance Officer in the offices of the Torquay District Hospital Management Committee (they managed all the local hospitals in South Devon) situated at Newton Abbot Hospital in East Street. It also served as the Registry Office for marriages, births and deaths – I can recall being asked to witness a marriage on several occasions. We were really busy with lots of Young Farmers' activities too – the organisation's changed since those days and members do lots of voluntary work now, which we didn't do.

With Anthony at a Totnes Young Farmers dinner and dance. That was my first evening dress and it was beautiful – light silver grey, with a wonderful floral pattern

At Wistmans Wood on Dartmoor the summer before we were engaged

We were engaged in March 1957 and married at St Mary's Church in Dartington on 24 October 1959. Anthony's cousin David was the best man, and my bridesmaids were my sister Ruth, my cousin Patricia Selleck and two little ones, Angela Badge and Elizabeth Pearse. It was a cloudy day, and it rained later – the reception was held at the Seymour Hotel by the bridge in Totnes (it's flats now) and we spent our honeymoon touring Wales in the blue A35 van.

We set up home in the flat attached to Merrypark Garage which was originally built to accommodate Anthony's grandfather Ernest and grandmother Annie on their retirement from Ponsworthy. When Annie died Ernest spent alternate months with Wilfred and Gwen and with Sidney and Florence. A couple of years later we moved from the flat to a cottage at Dunstone, where we spent the next ten years.

Left to right: Sidney, Florence, Ruth, Anthony, me, Adeline, Kenneth and Kenneth George

Left to right: Pat, David, Anthony, me and Ruth, with Angela and Elizabeth in attendance

With the lambs in a field at Dunstone, on Anthony's birthday in April 1958

Madge and Reg Harris lived next door but one at Dunstone Cottages, and were kind to us – she loved to knit, and made jumpers for our boys – and he spent a lot of his time in the garden tending a very large bed of rhubarb which they enjoyed eating every day. At specific times of day Reg's hobnailed boots could be heard tapping over the cobbles to his cider store in the shed opposite the cottage, where he would fill a large crack-lipped jug with the nectar – it was the real rough country type! Anthony was called upon twice a year to load the empty barrels into his vehicle, and together with Reg they would set off to the Crediton area for refills. He used to enjoy these trips, meeting the farmers and their cider business, and would arrive home only having dared to drink one glass. Reg was a little round man, and he so much reminded me of a rosy red apple!

With my mother-in-law Florence and Anthony and the family van (and collies Sharp and Rose) at Bittleford Parks in September 1958

Four-and-a-half years after we got married Stephen John made a very welcome entrance in our lives, followed two years later by Trevor Paul to complete our family. Both boys were christened at St Pancras Church in Widecombe. Anthony was a wonderful father – always there for them – he would just 'drop tools' and help them with questions and requests. He was never too busy. At the Thanksgiving Service held a year after Anthony passed away our elder son Stephen spoke about how his Dad always had time for his family.

One of Dad's favourite sayings – of which there were many – was, 'If you want something done always ask a busy person.' Tony Beard was that busy person.

When we were younger Dad's day began at 6.15am with a cup of tea and a couple

of Rich Tea biscuits to get himself going: out to milk the cows, back in for breakfast, then off out into the parish to do his milk round, back on the farm, lunch, then the afternoon spent on the farm hedging, saving hay, general farm work OR possibly opening a fête or giving a lunchtime speech, before milking again and in for supper.

Most days the evening hours were filled as Tony Beard, 'The Wag from Widecombe'. Off he'd go to some far corner of the Southwest to perform a cabaret show or two, an after-dinner speech, open an event, or a talk to a gathering, returning home late or even in the early hours. This was his routine about four or more days a week. A BUSY MAN!

This only changed when he decided to stop milking, and again when the cattle were sold off. DAD was retiring... but the diary of TONY BEARD told a different story!

Now any spare hours were soon filled with events... and getting involved with many organisations to promote and put Dartmoor, Devon and the Southwest on the map... This man never said 'No'; even in 2015, when his health was not 100 percent, Dad was still going out to speak at the odd dinner in his own unique way.

Even though Tony/Dad was a busy person he always had time to stop and talk to everyone he met, leaving them with a smile on their face.

This busy and knowledgeable man never forgot his family. HIS FAMILY CAME FIRST! He was always there for help and advice for my brother Trevor and myself as we grew up.

Eventually, when Anthony's mother Florence was taken ill, we all walked through the snow from the cottage in Dunstone up to Bittleford Parks to look after her. I remember that the snow was so deep we ended up walking along the tops of the hedges. Anthony and I never went back home to Dunstone again.

Florence died in 1978, two days before my father – it was a horrible time. Anthony's father Sidney lived with us at Bittleford Parks for a further fifteen years. He was a lovely old man – so kind. He even bought me a dishwasher, and was always willing to help: he used to say that I was like a daughter to him.

ABOVE Granny Florence Beard at Bittleford Parks in 1977
LEFT Trevor and Stephen in December 1966

LIFE AND TIMES

Farming and Family

First and foremost Anthony was always a farmer.

When he came home from college in 1952, his father had ten or twelve cows, a few bullocks, thirty sheep, a couple of pigs and a few chickens. Bittleford Parks was a typical small mixed Dartmoor farm of roughly 60 acres (later we did manage to purchase some more land to make it up to around 100 acres, including rented ground).

During the Second World War his father had been a Special Constable and was very lucky on one occasion. After one shift at Leusdon, he came home as usual. No sooner had he shut the back door there was a tremendous explosion: a bomb had been dropped on the very spot where he had been standing! To this day I have a piece of shrapnel from the bomb. In wartime farmers were asked to plough up fields that were normally under pasture – there were no concerns about the environment then – and grow potatoes and produce as much milk as possible. Every farm had a churn stand outside the gate, and a lorry would come from Daws Creamery at Totnes to collect the milk churns.

Anthony working on the farm, early 1950s

How farming has changed in the past fifty years or so was brought home to me recently when I was thinking about the dairy industry. During those years every farm, big or small, produced some milk, collected each day by the churn lorry, distributed by the Milk Marketing Board, and everybody seemed pleased with the system. The producer had a fair price, the distributors were happy and the consumer was content with the quality and the price.

Evidence of this past system is still seen in the countryside: the Milk Churn Stand. Outside every farm or at the end of the farm lane was a milk churn stand. What a variety of constructions there were – and many are still there to be seen today. So many people pass them unaware of what they are, or their historic value. I am certainly not suggesting that they should be scheduled, but it would be nice to preserve a few. Built at a height to be level with the lorry's platform, so that a full ten-gallon churn of milk, weighing about a hundredweight, could be slid across from stand to lorry without too much strain for the driver. In the bad winter of 1963 we had three lorries at one time stuck in our parish, due to the snow.

'Last Word' *Dartmoor Magazine* autumn 2009

Anthony at home with the sheep – Devon Closewools – in the early 1950s

Wendy with Deryk, David's son, in April 1960

Uncle Wilfred Beard at his garage at Merrypark, Widecombe, around 1960

His father Sidney was already delivering milk to some homes when Anthony came home from college in 1952, and by 1980 was supplying the whole parish with their daily pint, delivering on alternate days around Widecombe, Ponsworthy and Poundsgate (there were post offices in all three places). By that time we had Friesian and South Devon milking cows and we used the Artificial Insemination Centre at Dartington instead of buying a bull. When Anthony and I finally gave up the milk round and turned to a suckler herd we purchased a Hereford bull for the Friesian cows, followed a few years later by a Simmental bull. We had three Simmental bulls before we retired, and enjoyed travelling to various markets all over Devon to find the right bull to put on the cows.

Many people in the parish today remember Anthony's famous milk round. As the late David Beard once said,

Anthony had restless energy, leadership qualities and a determination to get things right. As he would say, 'If tid'n done proper nort 'appens.' This often led to innovation. He saw the need for a milk retailer in Widecombe. Soon he became the milkman for the whole parish. Sterilising milk bottles was an ordeal for a small dairy farm and so everyone was issued with a special jug and the milk was delivered in plastic containers. There were some mumbles of discontent but he was years ahead of his time.

Electricity came to the parish in 1961/62, and there was great excitement at the big 'switch-on'. SWEB had an exhibition in the Church House in the centre of the village with samples of refrigerators, cookers, fires and so on, and – most importantly –

washing machines, and of course televisions.

There were some real characters in the village then – where are they now?

One such character was Leonard Skinner, who lived at Glebe Farm, another farmer who supplied milk to some houses in the centre of Widecombe. He could be seen pushing a metal milk crate, mounted on old pram wheels and loaded with about ten bottles of milk, around the village green. He was a little man and always smoked a pipe.

Another was the post lady, May Harvey, who lived in the village and whose brother Andrew had a café beside the house, a galvanised building just down the hill from the Green. May could be seen behind the large counter in the room used for the post office, and there were always cats perched around the room, one often flying through the air and landing on the counter in front of the customers. The only other commodity sold were packets of biscuits. She was also in the church choir and was heard to say on festive occasions 'It's the wonsers today' in her broad accent. Of course she was

The Rugglestone Inn

referring to those parishioners who only came to church once a year for harvest festivals!

I can remember Widecombe Fair dinners being held there every year, with plates piled high with steaming meat and veg served to all of us, sitting at long trestle tables. The evening always ended with the carpet being rolled away and a good old dance – quicksteps, waltzes and Gay Gordons – with the music provided by a small country band.

At that time what is now The Café on the Green was a tearoom catering for the many visitors to the village who mainly arrived by coach. It was run by the Ulchin family. I don't remember Mrs Ulchin, but her two daughters, who ran the café after her death, I remember very well – two spinsters who could be seen pushing their two poodles around in a pushchair wherever they went. We even bumped into them at

the Devon County Show one year! In the tearoom money was never handled, being exchanged via a wooden spoon.

Another café in the village was called North Hall, which was demolished in 1987. Today on that site there is a tennis court and children's playground and an area for the local tug-of-war team to practise, besides many other sporting activities. North Hall café had a large car park, and coaches could be seen coming and going all day up and down Widecombe Hill. The Old Inn and the Rugglestone also catered for the many visitors that came to see the famous village. The Rugglestone, just down Sanctuary Hill, was run by Mrs Lamb and her daughter Audrey. There was no bar, just a back-passage-type room, with barrels of beer and cider. We used to deliver milk there – just a half pint, two days a week!

ABOVE And so to bed… Anthony, Stephen (aged three) and Trevor (about twelve months) – and teddies
RIGHT Trevor and Stephen in 1968, looking so grumpy! Madge Harris, who lived next door but one to us at Dunstone, knitted those little green jumpers for them

We certainly knew everyone in the parish at that time, and soon learned of any newcomers. The old people of the parish were always a bit wary of 'incomers' arriving; Anthony's grandfather used to use the word 'eddipeeps' to describe them, meaning they had come to Widecombe to hide away from wherever they had come from.

I often went with Anthony on the milk round, and used to do it on my own at busy times such as lambing and harvesting, or when he had to be away at an event. We met some very interesting people while we were out and about. One was an old lady living on her own in the Poundsgate area who did wonderful crochet work. She loved to chat when the milk arrived so she'd come out to see us and would stick her elbow through the sliding window of our Landrover, so it was impossible to move. It took a bit of Anthony revving the engine before we were able to move on – that's loneliness for you. And then there was the lady living in Lower Dunstone whose husband had died in the bedroom upstairs. She asked Anthony if he would go up and take a photo of him. Anthony flatly refused her request and told her to remember him as he was when alive. On the next milk drop she produced a black-and-white photograph of this poor man in bed with the sun shining through the window onto the iron bars at the head of the bed, resulting in the most ghostly picture – not a photo Anthony would want to keep!

Children's fancy dress at Widecombe Fair, 1969. Trevor won first prize – you can see him on the right in the flat cap

He was asked to do many tasks on the milk round, including picking up groceries and pensions at the post office for quite a few elderly people. There was so much trust in those days. His father used to say to him, 'Where on earth have you been all this time?'!

> *As any milkman or postman will tell you, through the job you become a member of the community you serve. With that comes a certain responsibility, such as noticing whether the milk or post has been collected or still on the doorstep next morning. If it was you would make sure all was OK. You might get involved with other things too, such as changing a light bulb, fitting a new fuse, or – especially with senior people living on their own – just lending an ear to a problem, and sometimes running the odd errand. In my own case I used to collect pension books on my travels, go to the local post office to collect the pensions, take them home and deliver them the next morning. You would not be allowed to do that today, due to all those PIN numbers and the associated lack of trust. Another 'job' came my way whenever there was a fundraising event in the parish. I would be asked to sell raffle tickets on my milk round (best do it on a Saturday when folks paid their milk bills, they'll have their purses with 'em then!). Not the best of ideas when you're running a business I can tell you, but I did it.*

Moorland picnic with the boys in 1971

On my milk round was a remarkable man who was also a gentleman – a gentile man – a man of principle. He was also a very devout Methodist, and this was brought home to me in a most amusing manner. On visiting this gentleman, Mr X, he would always say 'Mr Beard'. He had known me all my life and until I was twenty-one years old he called me by my first name, but as soon as I was twenty-one, I was Mr Beard. 'Mr Beard,' he would say, 'I am a staunch Methodist and I do not agree with drinking or gambling, but I will make a donation to the funds!'

I kept the money separate and would total it all up on returning home. I found that I had £1 more than the tickets sold. Ah! Mr X's, so I wrote his name on the counterfoil and that was done. When the raffle took place he won a bottle of whisky, which I duly delivered the next day. 'Mr Beard,' he said, 'I told you I do not gamble or drink alcohol, whatever am I going to do with a bottle of whisky?'

'Last Word' *Dartmoor Magazine* winter 2012

Anthony was shocked to discover a few days later that Mr X had used the whisky to kill the dandelions growing on the cobbled path in front of his house!

In the early 1980s a new headteacher, Keith Pearson, was appointed to Widecombe Primary School and with his young family arrived during a very cold and snowy winter. Their family included twin boys in arms, and they went to Ashburton to get

Christmas Bazaar, Leusdon Memorial Hall, 1972: Father Christmas visiting the local Badgers' Club. Stephen is fourth from left; Trevor and Susan second and third from right

some provisions. Next we got a frantic phone call from a very worried Keith telling us that they were stuck in the snow – could we help, as he didn't know how they could get back to Widecombe? So Anthony took our old reliable Subaru truck, loaded them into it, and managed to get them home without any mishaps along the way. It was a wonderful vehicle that seemed to be able to go anywhere, in any weather.

Anthony's father Sidney usually washed by hand all the returned milk bottles, then in the late seventies a wonderful new invention enabled us to use plastic bags instead of bottles. Great excitement! This amazing machine sealed each name-printed sachet, which came with a blue plastic jug with a hole in the bottom. The sachet was inserted in the jug and the corner snipped off so that the milk could be poured out. No more bottles to wash, and so a great time saver. Some older customers were a bit sceptical, and took a little time (with a bit of encouragement) to come to terms with all 'this new-fangled stuff'. I often stood and operated the machine: the sachets had to be inserted absolutely straight, or else disaster ensued!

We had moved into a new future; but in 1986 Common Market regulations stated that we could no longer sell unpasteurised milk to any shop, bed-and-breakfast or establishment where the milk would be sold on. Our milk came straight from the

On the milk round, early 1980s

cow, which is fine for use in an ordinary household. We looked into the cost of installing the necessary plant but decided that it was not feasible financially because of our small and scattered milk round. We used to travel sixteen miles a day, with ninety-two drops on the full round (Widecombe and Poundsgate). So that was the end of our retail milk round which had been built up over many years.

I can remember when in most villages a couple of petrol pumps could be found. There they stood complete with two glass vials, each of which held half a gallon, with a semi-rotary pump and handle. No electricity, just a smiling face of welcome – and you would get some real personal service. 'Shall I wash off the windows, Sir? Can

I take your oil dip, Sir? And what about your tyres? I'll test their pressure for you.' No self-service in those days: the proprietor was only too pleased to see you and do what he could to make your journey enjoyable. Personal service always.

When we bought our first tractor, it was a little grey 'Fergie'. A TEA Model I remember, and it ran on petrol. Petrol was one shilling and ten pence a gallon then (9p in today's currency). I well remember when petrol reached five shillings a gallon – Father had a fit then. 'Can't afford this' he said, so off he went and bought a diesel tractor instead. That was a lot cheaper to run…

Contrast all that with today. You try and find a filling station on Dartmoor – they are truly few and far between – and to top it all there are thousands more vehicles on the roads today than there were then. 'Tis another case of the big multiples killing off the small shopkeeper, village shop, corner shop, post offices and the rural garages alike.

'Last Word' *Dartmoor Magazine* autumn 2011

We then turned to beef rearing. We already ran a flock of Devon Closewool sheep, and an annual event was a trip to Blackmoor Gate on the edge of Exmoor to purchase a ram. We'd pile in the van and set off early for the trip to North Devon. Each ram was

ABOVE Anthony was very fond of Horace, a Simmental x Hereford bull which we bought after we stopped the milk round
RIGHT Anthony out birdwatching with Stephen and Trevor in 1974. He used to take them out on the moor whenever he could, telling them all about the wildlife and everything around them

scrutinised very closely and eventually a purchase was made, the ram loaded and brought home. It was a busy, busy life with haymaking, sheep shearing, lambing on cold frosty nights in the corner of a field, and all the general farm work. We never had holidays (I mentioned this to our two sons some years ago and they said they had a wonderful childhood and wouldn't have wished for anything different). But of course we did have days off for agricultural shows and special outings (after doing all the farm work first).

One particular episode worth mentioning involved the monks at Buckfast Abbey. Anthony and his father were carrying some bales on a trailer behind the tractor along the old road between Buckfastleigh and Ashburton when they noticed some monks in a Landrover waving vigorously to them. They thought, 'Gosh – the monks are very friendly today!', when it became apparent that there was smoke issuing from the trailer. Anthony quickly drove into a field (the gate being conveniently open), and jumped down to find the bales on fire. A spark from the tractor exhaust had set them alight. I don't know how he did it, but he managed to unlink the tractor from the trailer. The monks drove in behind them and quickly produced some Buckfast Tonic Wine from the back of their Landrover to help with the shock! As it happened our eldest son Stephen was passing at that time and realised that it was his dad's and granddad's tractor and trailer sitting in the field in a distressed state, so he rescued them and brought them home, accompanied by a box of Tonic Wine! A very kind gesture from the monks.

We had planned to retire and sell all the cattle in February 2001, when of course there was an outbreak of foot and mouth disease. We intended to sell them on the Monday, but on the previous Friday everything came to a standstill with a complete ban on cattle movement. What a strange time that was. Everywhere was so quiet, and Anthony stopped going to Plymouth for six weeks to do his radio programme because of the fear of spreading this terrible disease. There was a farm some miles away that burnt doubtful animals – what an awful smell it was, with smoke drifting on the wind. So it was another twelve months before we eventually fully retired from physical work on the farm, and now part of our land is rented out to neighbouring farmers.

I retired from being Secretary at Widecombe Primary School in 2001 too. I had been involved there for over thirty years, starting with just a few hours a week, mainly to collect the dinner money but ending up with an almost full-time job. I ended up taking dinner money from the children of children who had been at the school!

LEFT Four generations of Beards in 1993: Anthony, his father Sidney, Trevor and baby Oliver (ten days old) at Bittleford Parks

LIFE AND TIMES

Enter 'The Wag from Widecombe'

When Anthony was about four years old, he discovered that he could yodel, having heard someone yodelling on an old gramophone record. So from an early age – at local socials and concerts – he would be asked to yodel. He even composed a yodelling song in later years: 'When I first went to Austria'.

Dressed up for the YFC entry at the Babbacombe summer carnival in 1957

He performed in plays while he was at Plymouth College, and when he was with Young Farmers, and eventually became one of the founder members of the Moorland Merrymakers, which came about a few years after we were married. In 1965 the young wives of the parish put on a show to display what they had been doing at keep fit classes, and their husbands offered to help 'fill the bill'. So Anthony sang and yodelled, and told jokes. After the success of this first concert a pantomime was planned: *Aladdin*, written by his cousin David and the headteacher of Widecombe Primary School, Bob Bates. The ladies went to local jumble sales and made all the costumes from old curtains, bed covers, evening dresses and so on, and a local man put up £30 to fund the pantomime. He was repaid after the performances, and the group had £15 left in hand. Everyone had great fun at these gatherings, and a spring revue show in March was also started. The pantomime is still going to this day: quite an achievement for this moorland parish with its scattered population.

After appearing in the pantomime he was asked to tell a few jokes after a sheep breeders' dinner in Ashburton. His title of 'The Wag from Widecombe' came about when he was billed in a show in Ashburton put on by Gordon and Queenie Dumble. They named him as 'Tony', and it stuck. From then on if someone rang and asked for 'Anthony' we

Anthony at the spring show at Leusdon Memorial Hall in 1972. At that time the Moorland Merrymakers did a pantomime and a spring show. He walked right though the hall to the stage, and people really didn't know who he was. He always wanted to play that sort of part!

knew that person came from the time before his entertaining started, whereas 'Tony' was his stage name.

That was the start of his stand-up comedian act which was mainly directed at himself with tales of the misfortunes and funny happenings in farming. He dressed in an Oxford shirt, corduroy trousers tied with baler cord, a red spotted hanky around his neck and a waistcoat. To complete the outfit he wore black working boots and a trilby hat. But the full picture included a wonderful crooked stick, a hazel stick cut

'The Wag from Widecombe' in the garden at Bittleford Parks in 2008

from the hedge, much valued by Anthony and given to him by a farmer in Denbury, Lewis Pearse. He never went anywhere without this treasured stick and his ukelele banjo, which he strummed while singing. He always started and finished his act with a song, or a 'ditty', many of which he wrote himself.

He was spotted by an agent at one show and was immediately approached to do cabaret shows at many Torbay hotels, holiday camps, weddings and other special occasions, including medieval banquets. Soon he was travelling to North Devon, Cornwall, Dorset and as far afield as Bristol. I do remember one very funny time when he was asked to appear in Stratford-upon-Avon on Valentine's Day, and he wanted to travel back the same night. He asked a very close old schoolfriend and neighbour whom he had known all his life to help drive. This was the late Leonard Norrish, a well-known local man from Ponsworthy, and a very experienced driver and mechanic. Having reached the hotel in Stratford they were shown up to a bedroom for Anthony to change into his usual cabaret clothes. Suddenly there was a knock on the door and a trolley was trundled in, decorated beautifully with roses, food and drink and all the trimmings for a romantic evening! They absolutely fell about laughing. They never forgot this trip, especially as it turned out to be a very wintry, snowy evening for their travel home through freezing fog to Dartmoor.

Comedian   Compère   Entertainer
Cabaret, Stage, Radio and Television Artiste
Recording Artiste

The Wag from Widecombe
TONY BEARD

BITTLEFORD PARKS
WIDECOMBE-IN-THE-MOOR
NEWTON ABBOT, DEVON
Phone: Widecombe-in-the-Moor 246

He was invited to the Three Counties Show held in Sussex. He often performed with The Yetties, as well as with Jethro. Through the seventies and eighties he appeared every other Sunday in the summertime at Sandy Bay Holiday Camp, Exmouth, often with The Wurzels when Adge Cutler was in the group (sadly Adge was killed in a car accident, and Pete Budd later joined the group). The boys and I went with him (the boys learnt to swim in one of the swimming pools at the holiday camp). He also had a summer holiday booking with The Wurzels at Weymouth Pavilion. He entertained in many other holiday camps, in Cornwall and Dorset.

TONY BEARD
"The Wag from Widecombe"

Bittleford Parks
Widecombe-in-the-Moor
Newton Abbot, Devon
Tel: Widecombe 246 (036 42)

walkerprint
London 01-580 7031

ABOVE The Wag's first publicity photograph, late 1970s
RIGHT A publicity photo of Anthony with his dogs, taken in the early 1980s (Rover is on the right)

Another venue he frequented for many years was the Royal Seven Stars Hotel, Totnes, performing in their Old Time Music Hall, when the hotel was managed by Ken and Audrey Stone. Jean Richards from Torquay was the pianist and accordion player, playing background music while people dined. So many happy evenings were spent there; these appearances were very successful. Of course he was heckled every so often, but nothing gave him greater pleasure than coming back with a smart riposte. The Athenaeum Theatre, Plymouth, was another venue where he entertained on many occasions with Len Jackman, a well-known organist. For many years too, at Christmas and New Year, he did up to four cabaret spots a night, mostly in the Torbay area. Stephen often accompanied him to help with the driving from one hotel to the next, ending up at the Royal Seven Stars or the Holne Chase near Ashburton. Sometimes in the summer period he would entertain at two hotels in one evening!

Our younger son Trevor has some clear memories of 'my Dad, the comedian'.

I'm picturing a typical event perhaps forty years ago, going into a large, low-ceilinged social club, heaving with people, subdued lighting, but brighter at the far end where there is a small stage. It would be noisy, boisterous even, cigarette smoke mixing with the beer and the noise.

Dad'd be shown to a cubby hole to put on his costume: hobnailed boots, cords, an Oxford shirt, waistcoat with watch and chain, red-spotted neckerchief and battered trilby. And not forgetting the walking stick, crazily bent and his trademark.

He always felt the nerves – I could see them building as the time to appear approached – but then the call and on he went – grab the ukulele banjo, walk through the audience and into the spotlight.

Some crowds are harder than others, but most often his spot was a big, loud, joyous time for laughs and fun. He'd always start and end with a 'ditty', more often than not closing with his yodelling song; yodelling was just something he taught himself – very unusual, and people really loved it.

He had short routines of related jokes and chose what to use as he went along, driven by the crowd's reaction. He could build the atmosphere, his timing was perfect, so that the laughs rolled and built...

Dad would come off stage streaming with the exertion of it but happy, elated even on those nights. He'd connected with people in that crowd, and everyone felt so much better for it. All this he took forward into more general entertaining and presenting, but for me he was at the height of his powers when working the cabaret crowds.

Another publicity photo from the 1980s: The Wag driving a tractor!

Something else he did for many years was entertaining American tourists at the Manor House Hotel (now Bovey Castle) near North Bovey. This was arranged by Tauk Tours in the USA and consisted of a week's tour covering England and Scotland. On one occasion he even met a relation who was a descendant of a branch of the Beard family which had emigrated to America in the 1860s.

He often travelled to Bratton Clovelly to appear in many concerts organised by Brenda Yeo. Another event at which he acted as MC for many years was a big evening organised by Ian Huxtable in North Devon, where many artists were asked to perform in a large marquee and all proceeds raised were given to charity for Cancer and Leukaemia in Children. Many hundreds of people attended these shows, which included a wonderful supper. Ian raised many, many thousands of pounds for the charity.

I remember Renwicks Travel sponsoring Anthony and me on a publicity trip to Majorca. A week before we left Anthony, complete with our lovely old sheepdog, Rover, took part in a photo shoot at Exeter Airport. It was our first-ever flight, but despite some last-minute nerves as we walked across the tarmac to board the plane, we had a good flight to Magaluf where we stayed in large hotel with a swimming pool. A photographer took him around the island to all the popular tourist sites, taking photographs of him dressed in his 'Wag' attire. We were booked to stay a week, but because his father and the boys, who were quite young at that time, had to cope with the milk round and all the farm work, it was decided that we should make it for just four days. We arrived home having had a wonderful break. I have still got all the colour transparencies that were taken.

In 1976 Anthony was approached by Galaxy Records to record an LP, so arrangements were made to record live with a full audience at the Royal Seven Stars Hotel. It was a wonderful evening, each song being interspersed with a few jokes. The songs recorded were: 'County Show Song'*; 'I Wish I Was Back on the Farm'; 'Apple Cracking Time'*; Milk Producing Song'*; 'When I First Went to Austria'*; 'Tavistock Goosey Fair'; 'The Marrow Song'; 'Out Come Mother and Me'; 'Poor Poor Farmer' and 'Widecombe Fair'. His favourite songs – 'Out Come Mother and Me' and 'When Mother and Me Joined In' – were composed by Jan Stewer, alias A.J. Cole, who came from Torquay and was a schoolteacher. He wrote several books in the Devonshire dialect and Anthony has recorded many. In later years Anthony met his son, who told him that his father would have been very pleased with the presentation of his work.

*Anthony wrote these songs.

Working for the BBC

This all came about by accident... starting in 1975 with a phone call from BBC local radio asking him to sing the Jan Stewer song 'Out Come Mother and Me' over the telephone. A listener had asked the BBC to play it on a programme, so a request went out asking for details of the song. A listener phoned the station and said that Tony Beard was their man, so hey presto! – the next wonderful phase of his life began. The BBC phoned him and he sang the song down the line.

Next they asked him to come into the studio and sing the song, which lead on to an interview with David Bassett, the presenter of the lunchtime slot. After this live interview, two producers approached him and said they enjoyed listening to his voice and his Devonshire accent and could they use him sometime in the future. A few weeks later, David Bassett (who also ran a Sunday request programme) had to go into hospital and they asked Anthony if he would fill the gap for a couple of weeks. After that David told Anthony that 'he had made the request programme his own' and that he wished to step down from presenting it. Anthony was asked to do a short run of perhaps eight weeks.

When Anthony started his broadcasts, all the request programmes were recorded. One of the producers, Reg Brooks, showed him the ropes. I know it amazed Anthony how Reg edited the programme. For example, on one occasion Anthony introduced a record sung by Cliff *Richards* (of course it should have been Richard, without the 's'). Reg was able to take the tape and carefully cut out the offending letter. The power of a razor! When he'd been doing the programme for a few years, they let him to go 'live'. I've been in the studio when the programme was going out, quite often stifling a cough or sneeze and hardly daring to breathe. And all those buttons to control!

He did the programme for fifteen years before they issued him with a contract. He spent most of Saturday preparing for his Sunday programme, looking up reference books and picking out a subject about nature or any relevant festival information to talk about. He loved driving to Plymouth each Sunday and reading all the requests. People used to tell him about their lives, be they happy or sad, and would treat him as one of the family. He never forgot a lady from Tavistock who told him that she wasn't lonely any more because he came to lunch with her each Sunday, and he was amazed and humbled by how the audience used to allow him into their homes every week. He interspersed the music with talking about the countryside, a great love of his, and gave out notices of forthcoming events. He was joined in later years by an assistant, Darren Cox, and a firm friendship was formed. I'm sure Anthony would be thrilled to know that Darren is still involved with the Sunday programme today.

He was also involved with another weekly programme for Radio Devon: *Dartmoor Diary*, a fifteen-minute interview or talk about any subject to do with the moor. Some wonderful people came to Bittleford Parks, or he visited them at home to record the interview. Many of the different Radio Devon presenters who worked on the programme with him became good friends, as Pippa Quelch recalls.

I've been working at BBC Radio Devon for twenty-five years, and had the great pleasure of working with Tony for many of those years. I was one of a number of producers here to record BBC Radio Devon's Dartmoor Diary with him – where we travelled the moor and stopped to record features on aspects of Dartmoor history, geography and life. We've climbed tors and explored clay pits, stone circles and pig sties. We've trotted through bogs and navigated countless cowpats in torrential rain, sleet and snow... and with Tony as our guide we've loved every minute. He could always find something magical in the mundane and communicate it to an audience of thousands with the art of a truly gifted storyteller. It was why he was in such demand on both radio and TV over the years.

Tony loved to champion local food in the Dartmoor Diary. The day I met Tony, he served up hospitality 'Widecombe-style', known as 'Thunder and Lightning' – Wendy's bread, golden syrup and a huge dollop of 'clouted' cream. I liked him immediately! But woe betide anyone with the audacity to serve jam and scones with squirty aerosol cream! You soon learned to exercise a little caution in Tony's kitchen. One morning I arrived to find the table covered in mouse skeletons he'd picked free from a pile of owl pellets. Hunched over the tiny bones, wielding tweezers, Tony was in his element.

Perhaps one of Tony's greatest legacies was helping us see beauty in the everyday world around us – however small. A favourite Dartmoor Diary story was of the young family he met enjoying a day out on the moor above Widecombe. As he passed, he heard the children saying they were bored. 'How can you be bored?' said Tony, '...when there's so much to see right in front of you?' He told them to mark out a metre square of ground and showed them how to count all the plants and animals they found inside it. When he passed again much later, they were engrossed... and still counting!

I also presented the Sunday gardening phone-in with Tony, who had a feature called 'The Pest Desk'. It was a real joy to spend time with him – I didn't stop laughing or learning.

As a result of his radio appearances he was asked to appear on the local evening BBC1 television *Spotlight* programme. The producer would ring him up, requesting a song about any current news item for the following evening. I remember he wrote songs including ones about cider making, the Devon County Show, and the very dry summer of 1977 – for that they had him sat him in a bath, singing in his Wag's outfit! He used to compose many songs when he was milking the cows and write the words in chalk on the concrete walls of the shippon. He then learnt the words, usually accompanied on his ukulele, and would sing them straight to camera live; there was no autocue in those days. A nerve-wracking experience! On one occasion he appeared with Chris Denham at Tavistock Goosey Fair and was asked to sing the old song 'Tavistock Goosey Fair'. They were sat on a Big Wheel in one of those rocking seats – not his favourite ride! And then ITV also approached him too, and he ended up singing another song while leaning over a gate, with bales of hay for props.

Anthony with BBC Trustee Alison Hastings at the Frank Gillard Awards in Newcastle upon Tyne, October 2012, where he received the 'Outstanding Contribution Award'

His over thirty years of loyal service to local radio resulted in him receiving the Frank Gillard Award in 2012. He was flown to Newcastle upon Tyne where the national radio awards were being presented; he wasn't told why he was asked to attend, and I know he felt deeply honoured that his name had been put forward. He was presented with a bronze bust of Frank Gillard, a very prominent radio presenter for many years. A very great honour indeed.

He was asked many times to perform in a BBC television show called *The Big Time* presented by Esther Rantzen in the late seventies, but refused saying he was very happy with his life in Widecombe and had no desire to live out of a suitcase and travel the country.

Our friends, Neelia and Dennis Hutchins, ran a guesthouse at Leusdon Lodge, Poundsgate. They were always thinking of new ventures and in the late seventies they hit on the idea of holding medieval banquets. They asked Anthony if he would help and be Master of Ceremonies (MC) on these occasions, as Baron, with me alongside as Baroness. We were dressed in wonderful costumes made especially for the occasion. Anthony had very colourful attire finished with red tights and a beret-type hat made of velvet and satin. My dress was made of matching material (I don't think I would fit into it now!). We had some wonderful evenings there, with at least ten courses served with mulled cider and ale, with a red-hot poker being ceremoniously sizzled in a large ewer to warm the contents. People came dressed in costume and a very amusing and entertaining time was had by all, with Anthony introducing each course with jokes and the usual banter. A regular guest was a funeral director from Plymouth, known as 'The Earl of Plymouth', a little man with great personality who

One of the first medieval banquets at Leusdon Lodge. Oh – we had some fun there! Those were just makeshift costumes, but I'm wearing Anthony's great-grandmother's locket – I've got her earrings, too

At the Dartmoor Folk Festival in 2012

would love to chat with Anthony. He arrived with his wife and many friends in a large hearse-type car and was the life and soul of the party. Wonderful memories.

The Dartmoor Folk Festival at South Zeal was another great event in his calendar, held in August each year. Bill Cann, who started the festival, invited him to take over as MC for the Old Time Music Hall at the fourth Festival in 1981. This takes place in the main marquee on the Sunday evening and involves all the acts that perform over the weekend, often ending after midnight. Bill Murray (from whom he took over as MC), can't remember Anthony missing a single Music Hall until he retired in 2015. So on that Sunday, no sooner had he come home after doing his radio request programme for the BBC in Plymouth he grabbed some food and set off to South Zeal.

Bill says, 'There is no doubt that "The Wag from Widecombe" contributed a great deal to the establishment and success of this very special Dartmoor event.' He continues:

Tony would turn up at about 7pm, fresh as a daisy and by 7.30pm, with programme and running order in hand, he was ready to start. His welcome was always followed by a question to the audience such as 'Be 'e 'avin' a gude time my beudies?', then a short joke and after that "Haven't us got a wundervul lot of pervormers vur yur hentertainment this aivnin" and the first act (quick glance at programme) 'ees ...'

Right from the start, Tony would have the audience alongside him, and you could sense a beautifully relaxed atmosphere spreading over the entire marquee.

In the early days, the sound and lighting systems were set up and operated by the Festival Committee and things did not always run smoothly. On the one occasion that we chose to put the stage at the Dartmoor end of the marquee the sound cables picked up Radio One for all to hear. Tony managed the situation really well, singing a song that everyone could join in with while the problem was being rectified.

There were occasions when the entertainment went on until the early hours of Sunday morning. This never seemed to bother Tony and he always introduced all of the performers with the same enthusiastic spirit, never rushing them through in order to catch up on time.

He would tell a few stories between the acts and towards the end of the first half sing a song, perhaps 'I Wish I Was Back on the Farm', usually accompanying himself on the ukulele. He always had one more yarn up his sleeve to fill a gap when a stage change took longer than anticipated and whatever he chose to do, always went down well.

Dr Tom Greeves also has got Anthony's Folk Festival antics spot on:

For many years he was MC at the 'Music Hall' final evening of the Dartmoor Folk Festival, dressed in check shirt, red kerchief, waistcoat, corduroy breeches and boots, and carrying a gnarled and curvaceous walking stick. Here he would regularly sing and tell Devon anecdotes to an audience that he often reduced to near-helpless laughter. His timing was immaculate, his twinkling eye brim-full with knowing and sometimes wicked humour, and his smile melting even the stoniest heart. He was a consummate performer.

At the Dartmoor Folk Festival in 2014

Receiving the watercolour painting from Jason Rice, right, on behalf of the Dartmoor Folk Festival Association, with Mark Bazeley and me, in 2015

Kari McGowan's lovely painting

About six months before he died the Festival Committee gave him a lovely watercolour painting by Kari McGowan as a token of their appreciation for all the years he had travelled to South Zeal. I value it greatly, and have it hanging by the fireplace in the lounge at Bittleford Parks.

At the 2017 Dartmoor Folk Festival, with Trevor and Stephen. On the left are the Mayor and Mayoress of West Devon, Cllr Jeff Moody and Mrs Beverley Moody, and Shirley Bazeley, President of the Dartmoor Folk Festival Association. To the right is Jason Rice, Chairman

In 2017, accompanied by Stephen and Trevor, I was asked to open the Festival in Anthony's memory, which I was only too pleased to do. Four of our grandchildren – Oliver, Edward, Heather and Jeremy – performed two songs at the Music Hall on the Sunday evening. I was so very proud of them (and quite emotional). What chips off the old block they all are! They are quite accomplished musicians, and regularly sing and perform at events. Harrison and Lydia (Stephen's two) are also musical, playing the piano and singing with the guitar.

Another wonderful occasion came about when Anthony was approached by Creative Cow Productions, a touring theatre company which based most of its productions in Exeter and was directed by Amanda Knott, who lived on a farm near Exeter. The play was *The Farmer's Wife*, a comedy written by Eden Phillpotts in 1916 and made into a silent movie by Alfred Hitchcock in 1928. Anthony was cast as Farmer Sweetland with

Anthony in *The Farmer's Wife* at the Cygnet Theatre, Exeter in 2010. Next to him is Douglas Mounce of BBC Radio Devon, who died in 2013

the late Douglas Mounce as his 'wife', and Jo Loosemore (also of BBC Radio Devon) was in the cast too. Douglas was a famous panto dame and used to perform each winter in large pantomimes in Blackpool.

This play was performed at the New Theatre, Friars Gate, Exeter, from 27 August to 11 September 2010. It was a sell-out, and a resounding success. Anthony did so enjoy this experience – it was a real highlight for the Wag – and he often talked about all the fun that he and Douglas had (they knew each other quite well from both working at Radio Devon). He was dressed in typical garb of a farmer in 1916 and had small wiry glasses specially made by Vision Express to complete the outfit (they said that his own glasses were too modern). Dr Robin Wootton, former Chair

With the grandchildren on our fortieth wedding anniversary in 1999. Left to right: Oliver, Lydia, me, Heather, Jeremy, Anthony, Harrison and Edward

of the Devonshire Association (Anthony was President in 2008) said of him in his role, 'He was superb – much better than the farmer in either of the filmed versions... just a natural performer.'

Anthony travelled many miles to entertain at all sorts of events and venues, and he also did many evenings entitled 'The Dartmoor I Love' where he talked to various audiences about his life, interests and activities. He was also asked to chair debates and meetings. He had a very distinctive voice with a Devonshire accent which seemed to be very popular. He was the main speaker at the National Conference of Show Secretaries in Bristol in 2000.

He had some very funny routines and jokes, and was often asked to repeat them time and time again. He had the gift of good timing and of being able to judge his audience; if he felt the routine wasn't going too well he would change the act to suit everyone. Favourite jokes related to farming, doctors, holidays and going to market, as well as topical news. He knew so many jokes – I don't know how he remembered them all! Popular ones included seventeen cows, pig in a wheelbarrow, trains don't stop at Crewe on Wednesdays, buying a budgie... The grandchildren loved to hear his budgie joke, with all the associated antics.

He never had professional help with his scripts. When he first started he would come home and I would type out the routines while they were still fresh in his mind, so that he could avoid repeating the same jokes when revisiting venues. He usually started and finished each routine with a song, such as 'Poor Poor Farmer', 'I Wish I Was Back on the Farm', to name a couple. He also had DVDs made of all these songs.

Agricultural shows featured largely in his diary – Devon County, Chagford, Mid Devon, North Devon, Honiton, Okehampton, Totnes – besides many fêtes, garden shows and any event where someone was needed to open the proceedings. He was also asked to attend many vintage machinery events around Devon, and met some devoted vintage enthusiasts, and for many years he opened the Kingsteignton Ram Roasting Fair, held on May Bank Holiday each year. He came to know the roads of Devon very well, and just loved to be involved with activities of all kinds.

Anthony having his portrait painted in 2007/8. Shan Palmes, who used to live at Bonehill and gave art classes, asked him to pose for a portrait

LIFE AND TIMES

Coming Home

In May 1997 Anthony suggested forming a local history group to the then postmistress of Poundsgate Post Office, Margaret Steemson. She said, 'You call a meeting and I'll chair it.' So the Widecombe History Group was formed, and more than twenty-five people attended the first meeting. From that date to the day he died he was Secretary of the History Group. Many wonderful lectures and talks were given at the meetings held on the first Wednesday of each month, and there have been lots of walks on Dartmoor. Interesting excursions and trips have been undertaken, including a four-day excursion to Ironbridge in Shropshire with stops on the way in Bristol and Wales. We are still a very enthusiastic group and audiences of up to fifty people attend on occasions.

The History Group has published several books, including *All Along Down Along Widecombe Way*, *The History of Ponsworthy*, *Widecombe Fair*, *Widecombe Roll of Honour for The Great War 1914–18* and *A Devon Dialect Alphabet*. This last title was published after Anthony's death, but it was a project with which he was very closely involved. When one member of the History Group, Joanna Radford, an artist and expert in bookbinding and hand printing, heard Anthony reading out the alphabet

With members of Widecombe History Group at the launch of *A Devon Dialect Alphabet* at Widecombe Fair in September 2017

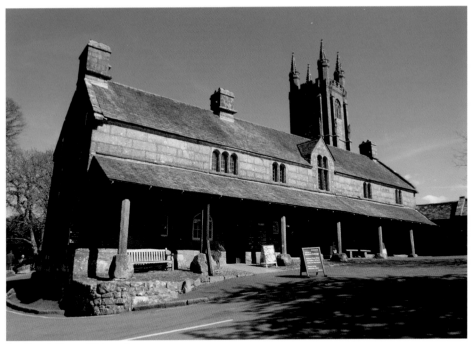

The Church House, Widecombe

rhyme at a charity lunch in his lovely Devonshire dialect, the idea of a book was born. Anthony had a copy of the rhyme written phonetically in Devon dialect, so Joanna set each letter and line of verse with one of her own original prints. She handprinted and bound three copies, but later did twenty more facsimiles. The three originals remain in the treasured possession of members of the History Group. Very sadly Joanna died a few months after Anthony, but she left the rights of the book to the History Group. With help from Joanna's family (particularly her son Nick, who works in publishing), and grants and support from a number of sources, the book was produced and launched at Widecombe Fair in 2017.

One great achievement of the History Group has been the digitising of all the old documents stored in the wooden chest kept for many, many years in the Church House, including lots of indentures which have been documented and made available on the internet.

Another project was making paperweights from the old lead removed from the roof of St Pancras Church in the village. First a mould was made by a retired engineer in Torquay, and then the lead was melted in an old saucepan. This all took place in our garage under the 'Team of Three': Terry French, John Kimber and Anthony. Talk about *Last of the Summer Wine*! One was cutting up the lead, one was

Anthony with Roger Whale and the new Two Crosses stone in 2008

in charge of the mould and the third stirred the saucepan. The end product was scrutinised and passed to me and my friend Mary to stick a green felt pad on the bottom of each paperweight to complete the job. Many hundreds were made and sold for £5 each, half the proceeds going to the church and the remainder to the History Group.

In 2008 Anthony played a big part in correcting a longstanding 'misnaming' on Southcombe Hill. The History Group was investigating the history of Widecombe Town Manor. A standing stone marks the manor's boundary with that of two others, Blackslade & Dunstone, and Jordan, at a point long known as 'Two Crosses'. History relates that the village lengthsman and council workmen annually recut two crosses into the turf at that point.

Over the years the spot had become known as Wind Tor car park, or

St Pancras Church, Widecombe-in-the-Moor

Dunstone car park, so in July matters were put to rights with the laying of a carved granite block, bearing the name 'Two Crosses' (and two carved crosses) at the appropriate spot (plus a 1p coin from 2008 for the benefit of future archaeologists). Roger Whale, chairman of the History Group at the time, donated the block, which had been lying outside his Ponsworthy cottage for a good fifteen years; it was carved by Andy Cribbett, Dartmoor National Park stonemason.

Anthony was also very involved in research to find all the names of those who fought in the 1914–18 war and compile the Roll of Honour for Widecombe. It was known that there had been one at Widecombe, but that it had somehow disappeared. It was discovered that forty-eight went to war from Widecombe, with six deaths, resulting in forty-two men coming home, of which three were Beards. Their names have been put on a scroll in Widecombe Church. There were five fatalities from the

1939–45 war, and their names are also found in the church. Fifty-six men from Leusdon went to the Great War with six fatalities; their names are recorded in Leusdon Church. He even asked Sue Viccars if she could take a photo of the Roll of Honour at St Peter's in Buckland in the Moor in connection with his piece for *Dartmoor Magazine* – not easy, since it is located high up in the apex of the porch ceiling (Sue says a ladder would have been useful)!

There were those who left their homes and did not return to their families and friends. Most towns and villages honoured the fallen with war memorials of various kinds – memorial halls, playing fields, crosses and even bus shelters, I have been told.

However there were those who did return, and to those too we owe a debt of gratitude. These rarely spoke of the horrors they had seen, or the atrocities they witnessed during that terrible period of history. They had to pick themselves up, dust themselves down and get on with life. Changed forever were the young men who left behind their families and friends to fight for 'King and Country'. There was no counselling when they came home, just a handshake: 'Well done chaps', go home and pick up where you left off! The best that most received was their name on a Roll of Honour hung in the church porch, and many of those lists were incomplete. Several soon deteriorated in the damp atmosphere. Some were renewed many years later and rehung inside their churches. Some, like the Widecombe Roll of Honour, deteriorated completely, were lost or disappeared. We need to commemorate their sacrifices and try our hardest to establish a complete list of all those names from every parish who so generously fought for what they believed was a just cause during those terrible years. Visit the church porch of Buckland in the Moor and you can find their Roll of Honour carved in wood for all to see.

Many sons of the 'well-to-do' families of Britain, often commissioned officers, did not return, and with no heirs to the large estates many were broken up, creating much distress to communities. Many of the old manorial systems disappeared and much history was forgotten and documents destroyed or lost.

The devotion of these men, some just boys, must never be forgotten… This was supposed to be 'the war to end all wars' – so what happened? In twenty-five years it started all over again…

'Last Word' *Dartmoor Magazine* autumn 2013

Another big research project undertaken by History Group members is on the site of North Hall Manor, situated in the centre of Widecombe. Three archaeological excavations have been carried out so far at the site of the moated medieval manor house, one of only a handful in Devon. Volunteers have assisted professional archaeologists in unearthing old coins, pieces of pottery and evidence of early buildings. Anthony was

Anthony with archaeologist Andy Crabb at the site of North Hall Manor in 2015

so very interested with this project, and spent many hours on the site. Peter Rennells (who Anthony used to affectionally describe as a 'blow-in' – only having lived in Devon for fifty years!) has done so much work into the history of the manor over the years, and he tells a good story about going with Anthony to give a talk about local history groups and North Hall.

Anthony once volunteered me to accompany him to a village deep in the South Hams. By giving a talk on one of our activities he was trying to encourage people to form their own history research groups.

For forty minutes, without script, he enthused about the possibilities yet to be discovered. Then he calmly announced, 'Peter will now tell you about a project he is working on.' Panic! I said to Anthony, 'I usually "do" the second half, after the tea break.' Big smile. 'Sorry, boy, but this lot don't have tea, they were at the sherry before we got here. Probably coffee at the end.'

Well, I am not ready. Bits of paper appearing from my pockets did not help the

Widecombe's restored Pig House – there's a seat inscribed with Anthony's name in the memorial garden

situation. I was forced to ad lib my way through the final forty minutes. However, with Anthony by my side, complete with stage whispers, I get through. Feeling rather ashamed of my contribution I try to keep a low profile, in the shadows behind a coffee cup.

Not Anthony: he does not do embarrassment. He has already covered the table with books on Widecombe Fair and Ponsworthy, plus a box of handmade paperweights. While he is taking the money, I am confronted by a military type of the old school. Fearing the worst, I receive a heavy pat on the back. 'Well done, good show what, better than Morecambe and whatsisname.' I convey this message to Anthony, who comments, 'A successful evening boy – we must do it again.'

And we did! – but never to the same formula.

He would be so pleased to know that the investigations are still going on – and that the old Pig House in Widecombe has been restored, too. He devoted many hours to the History Group and enjoyed all the meetings and outings. He was always interested in the manorial boundaries of the parish and had great knowledge about Widecombe history. He enjoyed contact with other history groups, often chairing the annual meeting of local history groups held each May at Parke, and met some very interesting people. He, with friends, led many tours around Widecombe village and I know much enjoyment was had by all involved. The Devon Women's Institute came for one of these tours, but because so many people turned up they had to be split into three groups on three different dates!

Another great interest of Anthony's was the Devonshire Association, founded in 1862 by William Pengelly of Torquay for the 'Advancement of Science, Literature, and Art'. The Association was presided over by many eminent and distinguished people including doctors, lawyers, solicitors, lords and clergy – the gentry of Devon. The antiquarian and folksong collector the Revd Sabine Baring-Gould was one of the first presidents.

Anthony was so greatly honoured to be asked to be President in 2008. I shall never forget his great pleasure on receiving that letter – he was so very thrilled. He loved the experience, travelling throughout Devon addressing the various branches of the Association and meeting so very many interesting members. I often went with him and he seemed to attract large audiences when addressing the various meetings. It's always a twelve-month appointment so after serving his term he was elected on to the Executive Committee, with meetings usually held in Exeter and

Bovey Tracey. He had been collecting the yearly Transactions for many years and he could often be found referring to items in them. When the meetings were at Exeter I used to go with him and we always started the day with a coffee in Ferns, then I enjoyed the day shopping while he attended the meeting. A lovely memory for me.

At the end of his term he was awarded with a plaque to mark his year as President, of which he was very proud. When the Devonshire Association's Executive Committee heard that we were working on this book, Tony Buller (Vice Chairman of the Exeter branch) sent us some comments about Anthony that came from around the table, which included the fact that he was passionate about the DA and mentioned it to outsiders on all appropriate occasions, and that he always wore his DA lapel badge, much to the shame of the rest of the committee members! They also remarked on the fact that he faithfully attended all Executive Committee meetings during his Presidency, and that to the best of their knowledge that was unprecedented. And finally that 'his dedication is unlikely to be seen again', which is lovely.

Dr Robin Wootton (a former Chair of the Devonshire Association, mentioned earlier) has much to say about Anthony during his time in office:

Tony was a DA member of very long standing, and greatly valued the Association and what it stands for – he accumulated an almost complete set of the Transactions from its foundation in 1862.

His active participation in the Association began in the spring of 2007, when he was an invited speaker at the Presidential Symposium of Anthony Gibson. His talk, on traditional farming on Dartmoor, was excellent and – of course – greatly enjoyed. The DA has a different President each year, elected at the Annual Conference in a different Devon town, and In June 2008, at the Conference in Bovey Tracey, Tony himself became the Association's President. He told us that he regarded this as a great honour, joining a long line of scholars and clerics, nobility and gentry. He was a memorable President, taking a particularly energetic role in the Association's activities which to a great extent established a pattern for subsequent Presidents. He gave talks to all the Branches and some of the special interest Sections during the year, and attended the meetings of the Executive. His Presidential Address at the Bovey meeting, on 'Farming through the years' continued the theme of his earlier talk and extended it to farming history in general...

The other formal responsibility of each President is to organise a one-day symposium on a subject which they choose and with speakers whom they invite.

Anthony proudly wearing his Devonshire Association lapel badge and his Widecombe Fair tie

Anthony with The Dartmoor
Society Award in 2004

Tony's, in County Hall in April 2009 on 'Telling the Dartmoor Story', was a huge success, with an audience of over one hundred. Tony chaired it in his inimitable way, and the afternoon ended musically with a performance by Paul Wilson and Marilyn Tucker – a first for a DA Presidential Symposium. His way of handing over to the next President at the 2009 Annual Conference was if anything even more innovative. Normally a dignified and formal moment, this one included an unexpected performance of 'When Mother and Me Joined In', and a promise that his successor, a very distinguished lady, should follow his example next year – in a distinctly less respectable way. The audience held its breath. Fortunately, she was very amused.

The Association owes him a great deal, and those of us who knew him remember him with the greatest affection.

And at the Thanksgiving Service, Dr Todd Gray, former Chair and President, said:

...for all of our 155 presidents, he proved to be one of the most successful, alongside such eminent men as Sabine Baring Gould and W.G. Hoskins. Former President Beard is remembered with great fondness... We have had presidents – both men and women – for whom Devon has been a happy accident, a brief part in their lives. But in Tony we had an individual in whom Devon sat at the core of his existence. And with it came sincerity.

The list of what he got up to goes on and on... In 2004 he received The Dartmoor Society Award, given annually to someone who has made a special contribution to Dartmoor. It's a lovely hand-crafted ceramic plate, engraved with the words 'For sharing his Dartmoor wisdom, empathy & wit'.

He appeared on the BBC's *Countryfile* programme and at *Children in Need* events. He was interviewed on radio many times: he seemed to be the first contact for anything connected with Devon, Dartmoor, the Devonshire dialect and Widecombe. He was contacted many, many times by both television and radio for interviews about Jay's Grave and Dartmoor legends. One of these was on Radio 4 with the politician Ann Widdicombe, together with our vicar, Revd Geoffrey Fenton.

He was asked to write the 'Tailpiece' in *Dartmoor the country magazine* for several years, for the then editor Hilary Binding. He continued with this when Sue Viccars took over as editor, and then in late 2008 Sue commissioned him to write the 'Last Word' for the last page of the quarterly *Dartmoor Magazine*.

Civic Service, Widecombe Parish Church, 1961. Left to right: Peter Hicks, Jim Hine, Wallace Whitley, Bill Miners, Bob Palmer, Mrs Miners, Lily Hambley (clerk), Mrs Robinson-Thomas, me, Dr Robinson-Thomas (Chairman Newton Abbot Rural Council), Anthony (Chairman Widecombe Parish Council) and the Revd John Brown

Visits to Ashburton Old Age Pensioners were always a popular event in his diary, and he also belonged to the Ashburton and Buckfastleigh Hospital League of Friends.

Anthony was the youngest Parish Council Chairman in Devon, when only twenty-five years old. He was a Governor at Widecombe Primary School for many years, audited the accounts of various local charities, and was Secretary to two very old Widecombe charities for over fifty years: The Widecombe Church House and Lands Charity and The Widecombe Education Charity. He was the contact for residents of the former charity's four cottages at Dunstone.

Contented observers at Widecombe Fair

He became a member of Widecombe Fair Committee at the age of sixteen, was Secretary and Agricultural Secretary for some time, and was the Commentator on Fair day (always held on the second Tuesday in September) for many years. Dr Tom Greeves talks about his 'rich Devon voice [which] could be heard over the tannoy system year in and year out at Widecombe Fair, reverberating around the valley and tors'.

Anthony's last appearance at Widecombe Fair was in September 2015, when he really wasn't very well. Our friend Lloyd Mortimore, who farms nearby at Lizwell, was primed to be on hand in case Anthony found it too much, but he was determined to manage the day on his own. Since then Lloyd, and Beryl Hutchings from Throwleigh, have taken over. As Lloyd says, 'There was no way I could emulate Anthony, so it was good to do something different. Beryl and I have got a good rapport – and our double act seems to work!'

Margaret Phipps, Chair of the Widecombe Fair Committee since 2013, has some lovely memories of Anthony's involvement with the Fair:

Anthony joined the Committee… back when only men were invited to be on it. He always laughed at the story about the time when, in 1980, the Fair needed a new Secretary. I thought that perhaps I could do that job. I broached the subject with the retiring Secretary who happened to be the local vicar but he was not too sure of that idea, replying, 'But you are a woman!'

Anthony went on to be Agricultural Secretary of the Fair for many years… He was also very involved with the schedule meetings. We would meet in someone's house, check through the schedule then have supper and drinks. It was another social gathering.

Anthony was always available when help with repairs and work on the Fair field were needed, more so in the days when jobs were done by hand, when he pared the hedges around the field with Ned Northmore. He went on to be Vice President in 2015–16. For many years too he was the Fair Commentator. He'd earned so much popularity from his radio programmes, and commentating at the Fair gave many people the chance to see him for real, up on the rostrum with a wonderful view of the Fair and Widecombe Hill beyond. His fans would walk past him and say, 'There he is!', and he'd always shake their hands if he could.

All they wanted was for him to say 'Hello there!' in his special voice.

What Margaret says about the way people reacted to him at Widecombe Fair is so true: people would just smile when he appeared. He loved meeting people, be they royalty

'Uncle Tom Cobley' and helpers at Widecombe Fair

– he met several members of the royal family, including HRH Prince Charles – or just ordinary working folk. He would take time to speak to anyone in a wheelchair or with any disability. He did many charity appearances, and often visited a Cheshire Home in Brixham and sang and told jokes to many disabled patients.

He was always saying, 'Your health is your wealth.'

He was sadly diagnosed with bladder cancer in January 2015. He persevered with all the different treatments and for a lot of the time carried on with his broadcasting and cabaret life. He never grumbled 'Why me?' or complained and after the summer and well into the autumn of 2015 was declared free of the disease.

During the summer he had been asked to attend a private occasion to tell some Dartmoor stories and so on at a large gathering in a marquee at Buckland in the Moor. He had finished his treatment and was in remission, so decided he would go. I was with him and during the proceedings he was asked to tell a few stories. He commenced his talk with a rather lovely story of 'The Devonshire Alphabet', told in the only way he knows… and that led to publication of *A Devon Dialect Alphabet*, which I've already talked about. This little book is a truly unusual and inspirational addition to anyone's book shelf.

At the end of November we went to the White Hart Hotel in Moretonhampstead for *Dartmoor Magazine's* thirtieth birthday cream tea party, a lovely occasion – it was so nice to catch up with some old acquaintances there.

Anthony with a Small Tortoiseshell butterfly in the garden at home in the summer of 2014: he loved all the wildlife around him

The surgeon just hoped that the cancer had not spread, but it turned out to be a very aggressive strain and at the beginning of December it was apparent that it had, and all entertaining had to stop.

I think you know the rest – Anthony passed away at Torbay Hospital on 30 January 2016, with myself, Stephen and Trevor beside him.

AFTERWORD

I shall never forget the Thanksgiving Service held for Anthony in Exeter Cathedral. Much as I would love to have used Widecombe Church I soon realised that it could never hold all the people that would want to come, and so Exeter Cathedral was chosen for the service. It was held one year after his death, and it took many months to arrange all the details.

Stephen and Trevor pay tribute to their Dad

Stephen and Trevor, who have been a tower of strength to me, and I had several meetings with the staff of the Cathedral who were all very helpful. Our vicar, the Revd Geoffrey Fenton, helped with the running order and I was very humbled by the Widecombe Bell Ringers who came to the Cathedral and rang the bells at the end of

Tinners Morris dancing outside the West Front of Exeter Cathedral at the Thanksgiving Service

the service – what a lovely thing to do. BBC television was there, along with several presenters from Radio Devon. Many of Anthony's friends gave wonderful tributes, and the Dartmoor Pixie Band and John Shillito's Jazz Band helped so very much. Anthony had told me many times that he wanted a jazz band to play at his funeral – no other details, other than he wanted it to be joyful. The Widecombe Singers, of which I am a member, gave a lovely rendering of 'The Widecombe Carol'. And four of our grandchildren played and sang 'Blackbird', by John Lennon and Paul McCartney, so beautifully. It was a truly uplifting Thanksgiving Service. The BBC was amazing, my friends and the whole village were so very supportive of the family – I shall never forget all their help and kindness.

I was quite overwhelmed by the number of cards and letters received after Anthony passed away. There were nearly four hundred really touching and personal tributes, which were of great comfort to me and the family.

How he had the stamina to work hard all day on the farm then change and rush off to all points in the Southwest and perform in front of audiences of anything up to a thousand people I don't know, but we, as a family, backed him up to the hilt – this special man, who filled Exeter Cathedral on 28 January 2017, really had a gift given to him. I know how amazed and humbled he would have been to see so many people there.

I must tell you about the headstone on Anthony's grave in Widecombe churchyard. We searched around the farm for a suitable piece of granite, then Stephen hit on the idea of using the granite milk churn stand, situated on the bank outside the bungalow against the road, which had been used many years ago when the milk was collected in churns by Daws Creamery of Totnes. It was just the right size, so we had it washed, engraved and erected – it's such a touching and personal tribute to a very kind and caring man who just loved meeting and talking to people and making them smile and of course, just living in this parish.

Last year, in 2018, the History Group held a special event in the summer in memory of Anthony – a picnic so everyone can sit around and have a good chat – and the plan is to make it into an annual event (in the Church House if wet). This year it was at Bonehill Rocks on a sunny day in the middle of a rather wet June. It's a very casual 'do', but I much appreciate the fact that everyone wants to remember him in this way.

IN LOVING MEMORY OF
'THE WIDECOMBE WAG'
ANTHONY ERNEST
BEARD
6TH APRIL 1936-30TH JAN. 2016
"Dartmoor was his home and life"

It has given me much pleasure to write about Anthony, my dearest husband for over fifty-six years, who is still greatly missed. He had such a diverse lifestyle: a Dartmoor farmer, an entertainer and a broadcaster.

My dear mother was quite right about him: 'He [had] been given a great gift.' We have two sons, two daughters-in-law and six very special grandchildren of whom he was so proud.

He often used to end his cabaret shows with: 'If you've found something you plan to do tomorrow don't put it off 'til tomorrow, do it today – because if you do it today and enjoy it you can do it all over again tomorrow!'

ABOVE History Group picnickers, June 2019
LEFT Anthony's grave at St Pancras Church

ABOVE The first outing of 'The Strollers', near Bowerman's Nose in May 2018. We try to meet once a fortnight on Wednesday for a walk, coffee and a catch up (left to right: Kirsty, Margaret, Aileen, Mary and me)
LEFT At the 2019 History Group picnic (held annually in Anthony's memory) at Bonehill Rocks

LAST WORD

And so we end where we began, at Anthony's Thanksgiving Service. Extracts from many of the tributes given at the service appear throughout this book, but there is one more rather special one still to come. We'd like to give the very 'Last Word' to Lloyd Mortimore, good friend and neighbour at Lizwell Farm, a mile or two away from Bittleford Parks. His eulogy says it all.

Whether it be Anthony, or Tony, we're all here today to celebrate the life of, and the legacy left by, one very special person. To so many of us he was a special friend, neighbour and a mentor.

As a Friend, he was someone you could always confide in and be assured of a carefully considered and open-minded opinion. He appreciated the value of taking 'time out' for people. He liked nothing better than 'chewing the fat' with a friend, and you knew that you would be more enlightened as a result.

As a Neighbour, I was lucky enough to live next to Anthony for over sixty years. He was an infectiously cheery neighbour, being dependable, interested and, as you can imagine, always armed with a quick quip. It's funny how you miss the simple things… I miss seeing his sports jacket draped over the back of his chair in the kitchen as I drive past Bittleford Parks. It always gave a warm confidence that he was in residence! It's not there now.

As a Mentor he encouraged many of us to share his love for the Young Farmers and the Moorland Merrymakers, our local amateur dramatics group formed by him and Wendy, together with those other young couples back in 1965, as a spin-off from a young wives' keep fit group when the winter nights were long and there was only one channel on television! Who would have thought, then, that there would later be a 'connection' with the BBC?

These two groups have been instrumental in moulding the characters and direction taken by so many of us in and around Widecombe. Anthony was a former Chairman and Club Leader of the Newton Abbot Young Farmers' Club, and thereafter a lifelong supporter. Leusdon Memorial Hall has been the home of the Moorland Merrymakers for more than fifty years, and the laughter that has been generated in their name has made Dartmoor a better place.

Now I don't know about you, but I think that we should consider rewriting the history books! Cause I reckon that if Tom Cobley's mates all squared up a little bit

*there would be room on the back of that mare for Anthony as well… and as they ride
by you could hear him call out his infamous 'Ullo there!'*

*I would like to leave you with a thought that I feel echoes the respect, love and
affection that our community holds for Anthony.*

Tone Beard, Tone Beard, now where 'ave 'ee gone?
'Ees all along, down along, out along lea
Us be missing your voice, us be missing yer zong
'Ees… wi' Bill Brewer [etc]

For vifty years, the vace of the moor
'Ees all along, down along, out along lea
With vame and good fortune – but to us so much more
'Ees… wi' Bill Brewer [etc]

Now tiz time for a rest, at the end of the day
'Ees all along, down along, out along lea
But you'll always be special, down Widecombe way
Now you're wi' Bill Brewer, Jan Stewer, Peter Gurney, Peter Davy, Dan'l Whiddon,
  Harry Hawke
And Uncle Tom Cobley and all, and Uncle Tom Cobley and all!

Widecombe's Uncle Tom Cobley model, which can be seen in St Pancras Church, was found in pieces in Cornwall and ended up in our garage before being restored! Its first appearance was at Widecombe Fair in 1959, after which it disappeared; it was back at the Fair exactly fifty years later

ACKNOWLEDGEMENTS

Thanks are due to so many people who have sent us their memories of Anthony or who have helped with photographs. We would like to thank the following (in alphabetical order): David Ashman, the late David Beard, Stephen Beard, Trevor Beard, Tony Buller, Aileen Carrett, Peter Carrett, Chris Chapman, Todd Gray, Tom Greeves, Lloyd Mortimore, Bill Murray, Margaret Phipps, Pippa Quelch, Alan Quick, Peter Rennells, Rob Steemson and Robin Wootton.

WB & SV

Most of all I would like to thank Wendy for so generously sharing the story of her life with Anthony with all of us.

SV

PHOTOGRAPH ACKNOWLEDGEMENTS

THE BEARD FAMILY pages 3, 9, 14, 15, 16, 17, 18, 19, 20, 21, 22, 25, 26–7 (Devon Commercial Photos), 29, 32–3, 34, 35 (top *Western Morning News*, bottom *Torquay Times*), 36 (HR Rivers, Chudleigh), 37, 38 (*Torquay Times* and Devonshire Press Ltd), 39 (top), 40, 41, 42, 43 (Reginald A. Baker Press and Commercial Photography, Exeter), 44, 45, 46, 47, 48, 49, 50–1 (*Torquay Times*), 52, 53, 54, 55, 58, 59, 60 (*Western Morning News*), 61, 62 (Torquay West of England Newspapers), 64, 65, 66, 70, 71, 73, 74, 75 (*Western Morning News*), 77 (*Express & Echo*), 81 (© BBC), 82, 88–9, 91, 110–11, 113 (*Mid Devon Advertiser*/Steve Pope)

© CHRIS CHAPMAN PHOTOGRAPHY pages 6, 104

SUE VICCARS pages 10, 12–13, 31, 39 (bottom), 56–7, 72, 92–3, 94, 95, 96, 97, 100, 107, 109, 114, 116, 120, 124, 126–7

© SKI HARRISON PHOTOGRAPHER page 62

ALAN QUICK pages 68–9, 83, 84, 85 (top), 86, 87

KARI MCGOWAN page 85 (bottom)

TOM GREEVES page 99

DEVONSHIRE ASSOCIATION page 103

AILEEN CARRETT page 117

PETER CARRETT pages 118, 119

View across Widecombe towards Bonehill Rocks and Haytor